YOUR KNOWLEDGE HAS VALUE

Anita Theis

3M Case Analysis: Cultivating Core Competences

GRIN Verlag

Bibliografische Information der Deutschen Nationalbibliothek:

Die Deutsche Bibliothek verzeichnet diese Publikation in der Deutschen National-
bibliografie; detaillierte bibliografische Daten sind im Internet über http://dnb.d-
nb.de/ abrufbar.

Imprint:

Copyright © 2012 GRIN Verlag GmbH
Druck und Bindung: Books on Demand GmbH, Norderstedt Germany
ISBN: 978-3-656-35192-4

This book at GRIN:

http://www.grin.com/en/e-book/205966/3m-case-analysis-cultivating-core-compe-
tences

GRIN - Your knowledge has value

Der GRIN Verlag publiziert seit 1998 wissenschaftliche Arbeiten von Studenten, Hochschullehrern und anderen Akademikern als eBook und gedrucktes Buch. Die Verlagswebsite www.grin.com ist die ideale Plattform zur Veröffentlichung von Hausarbeiten, Abschlussarbeiten, wissenschaftlichen Aufsätzen, Dissertationen und Fachbüchern.

Visit us on the internet:

http://www.grin.com/

http://www.facebook.com/grincom

http://www.twitter.com/grin_com

3M Case Analysis:
Cultivating Core
Competence

Anita Theis

Table of Content

1

Introduction

The following report assesses the strategic performance of 3M in 2006 by evaluating its core competence, its competitive advantage and its strategy used to reach 3M's mission which is defined as "*Solving and delivering unique solutions for original equipment manufacturers and mass channel customers*". This analysis brings forward a set of recommendations, consisting of an integrated set of actions which will exploit the company's competences more efficiently and therefore maximize value and enhance the company's strategic competitiveness in the future.

3M's Core Competency

To be a successful business, a company needs to develop core competences and base its strategies and its products on those. Core competences are defined as the collective learning within the organization; especially about the coordination of diverse production skills and the integration of multiple streams of technologies (Prahalad&Hamel, 1990, p. 82). These competences are business processes that fulfill the following criteria:

- Provide potential access to wide range of markets
- Contribute to the perceived customer benefits of the end product
- Difficult for competitors to imitate

Furthermore, one important aspect of core competences is that they do not diminish with use (Prahalad&Hamel, 1990). The connection between competences and a company's end products can be seen in the following graphic:

Graphic 1 - Competencies: The Roots of Competitiveness

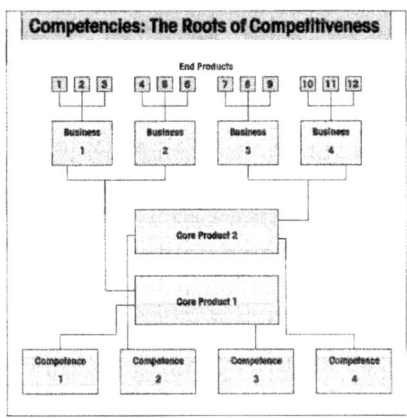

The corporation, like a tree, grows from its roots. Core products are nourished by competencies and engender business units, whose fruit are end products.

(Prahalad&Hamel, 1990, p.81)

2

In the case of 3M, their core competences are being innovative and creating synergies between different industries. The company has a "*unique model of a technology and manufacturing adjacency lattice that shares basic technologies and manufacturing processes across multiple businesses, markets and product lines*" (Case 3M).

Most of 3M's basic businesses are connected to each other in this way rather than being isolated from each other, therefore basing all of their products on their core competences.

3M's Sustainable Competitive Advantage

A competitive advantage exists, "*when a firm is implementing a value creating strategy not simultaneously being implemented by any current or potential competitors. A firm is said to have a sustained competitive advantage when it is implementing a value creating strategy not simultaneously being implemented by any current or potential competitors and when these other firms are unable to duplicate the benefits of this strategy*" (Barney, 1991, p.102).

This definition is based on two assumptions:

- Resource heterogeneity, and
- Resource immobility

Following from this, a company can obtain a sustainable competitive advantage, if it operates in a market/industry in which resources are heterogeneous and immobile, and its resources are valuable, rare, imperfectly imitable and non-substitutionable.

Graphic 2 - Relationship between Resource Heterogeneity, Resource Immobility, VRIO and sustained competitive advantage

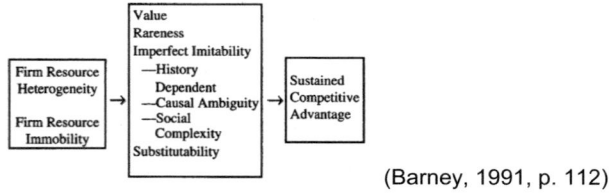

(Barney, 1991, p. 112)

3M's sustainable competitive advantage is based on their capability to combine scientific, engineering and manufacturing competency throughout different technology platforms in order to serve their niche markets. Within those technology platforms 3M has gained a tremendous knowledge and is able to use this comprehension to develop new products for different markets. Thereby a huge amount of linkages are formed between each technology platform and each market. This cross business enables 3M an internal technology transferring and sharing.

To test the potential of 3M's competitive advantage Barney's VRIO framework is used.

3

Valuable:

The value of the technology exchange is reflected in boosting innovation. Thus one technology platform can generate profits in different industries. In reverse, one market can benefit from the expertise of varying technology platforms. This provides a high value for 3M's competitive advantage.

Rare:

There is a necessity for high financial recourses to secure the rareness of this competitive advantage. Therefore, only large companies are potentially able to enter this monetary commitment. The rareness is hence given.

Imperfect Imitability:

This complex system of technology exchange among several markets is due to the experience of over 100 years. During this period the coordination was further developed and adapted according to the market situation and needs of the company. The history of depended condition leads to an imperfect imitability.

Organization:

From the organizational point of view 3M has built its company to support the technology exchange in the best way. However, there is still potential available for further improvements when it comes to the efficiency of the logistic structure of 3M (out of a theoretical point of view).

Reviewing the VRIO framework one can say that 3M has an unexploited competitive advantage. But since a perfect organizational structure can be hardly performed a sustainable competitive advantage can be awarded.

External Environmental Forces

3M is an international company, which is not only active in its domestic market in the United States, but also all over the world where 3M is generating more than 60% of its sales in mid-2006. Therefore, it has to cope with global issues and global environmental forces, especially since the company decided to concentrate on countries like Russia or China for its international growth. However, these countries and markets bear some political and legal issues and challenges. In order to get the best out of exploiting its core competencies and strengthening its competitive advantage, 3M has to be aware of the existing external

4

environmental forces as these might have strategic implications in the future. The factors in questions are summarized in the following table.

Table 1 - External forces tht impact 3M's future strategy

	Which forces?	Strategic implications
Political	- Countries like China and Russia have a higher percentage of bribery related to local authorities leading to an increase of complexity and insecurity	⇨ 3M has to analyze cultural settings in order to analyze these delicate areas and to be aware of all the practices and the ways to operate
	- A company producing in China has to be at least partly owned by a Chinese enterprise leading to the necessity of joint ventures	⇨ A weighing up of benefits and risks is required
Economical	- High oil prices	⇨ Developing a purchasing department for flexible supplying partners
	- Rare earth monopoly in China	⇨ Setting up new manufacture methods in order to avoid shortages
	- Uncertainties linked to exchange rate fluctuations	⇨ Hedging in order to minimize exchange rate fluctuations
		⇨ Forcing business partners to proceed the transaction in Dollar
Social	- 3M has penetrated many markets and so has to deal with different cultures and customers that have different needs and expectations	⇨ Providing a cross cultural program, which involves several actions to improve the understanding of different cultures
	- Involvement of customers' expectations	⇨ Developing a direct responds program from the customer to adapt products to their needs
Technological	- In a context of high competitiveness, the technological environment advances quickly	⇨ The market requires a constant technological surveillance.
Environmental	- Global warming, and rising awareness of customers regarding environmental friendly	⇨ 3M should reform a greener manufacturing process in order to

5

	practices		decrease CO2 emission and develop a green brand marketing strategy
	- Impoverishment of natural resources	⇨	3M has to think about substitute materials to manufacture their products
Legal	- In Russia, China or other emergent countries there are less opportunities for protecting intellectual property rights	⇨	In these markets, 3M has to put more effort in order to defend its innovation level and to protect its patents

For 3M, especially the economic factor is important as the company depends on oil and the rare Chinese earth resources. For the future it is important that 3M develops innovative technology in order to not depend on oil and earth, to use it more efficiently or find substitutes.

3M's Strategy

3M's mission is *Solving and delivering unique solutions for original equipment manufacturers and mass channel customers.* In order to live up to their mission, 3M uses a differentiation strategy by developing a wide and diverse breadth of technologies, that – combined together – create a steady stream of groundbreaking products, which can be charged a premium price for. This creation of synergy is used in a sequential entry strategy: 3M develops resources and technologies for one product in one market and then use this technology to enter new markets from a position of strength. 3M however needs constant growth and a very innovative team to keep their market share. As growth can either happen via organic growth or by acquisition, 3M has put a big effort into acquiring other companies in order to diversify and launch new products.

3M's Acquisition Strategy

3M first started to acquire larger companies to gain knowledge and market shares. For example, 3M acquired Corning Precision Lens Inc. in 2002, to become the world's leading supplier of optical lenses (Case 3M). However, 3M changed its strategy to acquiring mainly small companies nowadays. Reasons for this lie in the assumption, that organic growth is more difficult and expensive and only leads to incremental growth while acquisition create rapid growth and ensure the company's market share. It is however important to keep in mind, that acquisitions are also risky and costs can increase easily.

Through acquisition, 3M gains excess to human capital and to new products and technologies. This supports their product range, as well as it gives 3M employees innovative

6

ideas for new products by collaborating with new people. Therefore, 3M's acquisition strategy supports its core competence. Furthermore, by acquiring small companies in different industries - instead of larger companies - 3M supports its diversification strategy. Diversified investments lower the risk of failure and increase the possibility for future success. Another positive effect of acquiring small companies is that these are easier to integrate into 3M's organizational structure, due to the fact that small companies usually have a less hierarchical and more bottom-up organizational structure.

Negative aspects of acquisitions are that, they can become rather expensive, especially, when acquiring companies from a foreign country. Combining two different cultures is also a challenge of acquisition.

The acquisition strategy of 3M's seems a bit random, when seen from the outside. 3M is acquiring small companies, which occur due to a "garage idea" of which 3M does not know if their investment will pay off in the future. However, they have the strategy of acquiring small companies, instead of risking that those will become a strong competitor in the future.

3M should stick to acquiring small companies for the reasons mentioned above, however, they have to focus on keeping up their own in-house innovation instead of focusing only on gaining innovative products or technologies from acquired companies.

Recommendations

In order to strengthen its competitive advantage and to maximize value, 3M needs to exploit its core competencies more efficiently. The core competence, that the competitive advantage is built on, is innovation and the creation of synergies between different industries, the company is operating in.

The following paragraph will describe a set of commitments and actions recommended in order to increase the company's performance.

Fostering Innovation

3M is positioning itself as an extremely innovative company, offering different opportunities for its employees to act innovative. It can however be seen, that the innovation processes can still be improved in order to reach their full potential. When James McNerney became 3M's CEO in early 2001 he launched a couple of initiatives that slowed down innovation, including the layoff of 6,500 workers for cost-cutting reasons. A company, in which 6,500 employees suddenly lose their jobs might have difficulties creating a culture in which errors are tolerated and knowledge-sharing encouraged, as employees have to fear for their job and try to gain an advantage due to knowledge asymmetry towards their co-workers. Furthermore, McNerney launched an initiative called "3M Acceleration" in order to be able to get the best products to market much fast. This however also led to the fact that a lot of ideas got dropped before their full potential could possibly be reached. This might lead to a de-motivation of employees to act innovatively, as they might feel that their effort and ideas are not valued by management.

The most important challenge for management in order to enhance performance should be fostering innovation by re-gaining the trust and commitment of its employees into innovative thinking. Key factors for that are motivation and organizational support (Elfring, 2005), that can be divided into the following aspects that the company can influence: Culture, Organizational Structure, Management Support, Rewards and Reinforcement.

Creating an innovative Culture[1]

3M has defined its culture as a "Culture of Innovation", allowing employees to take-risks at the same time as mistakes are tolerated. With their 15% rule, employees are encouraged to work independently on other projects with different people, creating active knowledge sharing and independent thinking. It is recommended that an innovative culture can further be developed by creating open work spaces in which communication is encouraged.

Having a bottom-up Organizational Structure / Management Support

3M operates a bottom-up structure, making it possible for the employees to not only have a voice within the company, but also to – to some extent – influence the strategy and the plans being implemented by middle- and top management. If management encourages its employees to believe that innovation is part of the role set for all members and shows their support in their employees' contribution to innovation, employees can be more motivated to bring ideas forward and work on experimental projects (Hornsby, et al., 1993).

By introducing a meeting once every two weeks or every month between Management and working groups, in which employees can present their ideas or projects they are working on during their "15% rule" increases the rule's potential, as the employees actively feel that management cares about their work and therefore feels more encouraged to be innovative. Furthermore, top management can show their contribution by setting up coaching programs, in which employees can benefit from senior managers' experience, their knowledge and their network. Coaching is also an important aspect in balancing exploiting and exploring activities (Elfring, 2005).

---

[1] An innovative culture can be described by the degree to which it encourages communication and information sharing, the degree to which it is open to new ideas and the extent to which it provides an environment that views innovation as critical to the company's competitive position. An innovative culture tolerates risks and failure and encourages employees to experiment with new ideas (Elfring, 2005; Hisrich, 1990).

8

Rewards/Reinforcement

Rewards and reinforcement increase the motivation of employees to engage in innovative behavior. Innovative employees should be appropriately rewarded for both the energy and the effort they put into the creation of a new idea. By increasing 3M's employees' responsibilities and challenges, and at the same time acknowledging their ideas, the management team can further motivate them to act innovatively (Hornsby, et al., 1993).

Efficient Creation of Synergies

Even though some of the initiatives that McNerney introduced when he took over the company in 2001 hindered innovation to some degree, it must not be overseen how important efficiency for 3M is and how those initiatives helped the company to increase revenues. 3M operates a sequential entry strategy into new markets by developing and exploiting resources in one market that then can be transferred to other products and other markets, as the use of central technology is encouraged throughout businesses. These synergies created are a main reason for 3Ms competitive advantage and are based on knowledge sharing – an essential managerial challenge that requires the introduction of a knowledge management program within the company in congruence to the creation of an open-innovation-based corporate culture.

Conclusion

The assignment showed how important it is to focus on core competencies to be successful. In the case of 3M the core competences are being innovative and using synergies in different industries. Furthermore, it is also important to have a sustainable competitive advantage. This makes the difference between the competitors. 3M has an unexplored sustainable advantage. By becoming more efficient this can turn into a sustainable competitive advantage.

Being a global company make growth very difficult and expensive. 3M uses acquisition of small companies to grow rapidly and to gain more knowledge and expertise.

Since 3M is operating in many different markets, a lot of environmental factors are influencing 3M. As these economic factors are influencing all industries, they have a significant influence for future implications. The main challenge for 3M in the future is getting less depended on oil and rare earth. It should use its innovativeness to find potential substitutes. Furthermore, for staying as successful as 3M already is and becoming even more successful, it needs to increase its efficiency and its innovativeness.

Sources

Barney (1991). Firm resources and sustained competitive advantage. Journal of Management 17(1): 99-120.

Case 3M

Corporate Website of 3M. A Culture of Innovation
http://solutions.3m.com/3MContentRetrievalAPI/BlobServlet?lmd=1321384592000&locale=e n_WW&assetType=MMM_Image&assetId=1319209959040&blobAttribute=ImageFile ; retrieved September 20, 2012

Elfring, T. (2005). Dispersed and focused corporate entrepreneurship: Ways to balance exploitation and exploration, In Tom Elfring (ed.) Corporate Entrepreneurship and Venturing, Springer, 1-21.

Hisrich, R. (1990), Entrepreneurship/Intrapreneurship. American Psychologist, Vol. 45, Issue 2, p. 209-222 1990.

Hornsby, J. S., Naffziger, D. W., Kuratko, D. F., & Montagno, R. V. (1993). An interactive model of the corporate entrepreneurship process. Entrepreneurship: Theory and Practice, 17(2), 29-37. Baylor University.

Prahalad & Hamel (1990). The core competence of the cooperation. Harvard Business Review, May/June: 79